THE WALKING
MIRACLE

———∽∿∿———

Keep striving for ultimate
greatness!

THE WALKING MIRACLE

HOW THE 'SHORELINE RUNNING MAN' OVERCAME THE
INJURY THAT STOPPED HIM FROM RUNNING

—m—

LAMONT J. THOMAS

WITH

ASHLEY M. GRAHAM

WARD STREET PRESS · SEATTLE

The Walking Miracle
ISBN: 978-0-9844969-7-6

BOOK & COVER DESIGN BY VEE SAWYER

Dedication

Tina Tshering, Soname Tshering,
Shoreline Chiropractic, Brian MacKay,
Chris MacKay, Anthony Castano,
Alexander Canstano, Mark Dunlap,
Bridgett Linville, Andre Burshaine,
Daniel Nguyen, Davante Myles, DR
Greg Mack, David Ishkanov, Daniel
Ishkhanov, Simon Mengistu, Eddie
Nicholson, Mike Seely, Cary Seely, Evan
and Veronica Cataline, Hanna Ritchie,
Makenna Mae, Jaeda Lin, Julie and John
Cake, Bonnie Murdock Brayden, Patric
Brayden, Lina Jessen, Hazel Jessen,
Paisley Jessen, Jenni Wilson of Beach
House Greetings

Contents

THE WALKING
MIRACLE

L. A. Times

I bumped into a lady in a local coffee shop who happened to be ordering coffee before me. As a well-known person in the community, I started up a conversation, telling a short snippet of my story. She had seen me for years running, and as I told her my story, as I do with majority of the people I see in my community, she mentioned she knew of a writer/contributor to the *Los Angeles Times* newspaper, who might be interested in my story.

Mind you, I'd never been in a major newspaper before, and I was very cautious in my excitement. Not even twenty-four hours later, I received an email from Mike Seely. He wanted to do a story about me. I was in a state of shock, at first, but as we continued to communicate, I realized I had been handed an opportunity to reach others far beyond my own community. So Mike did some digging to verify that everything I was stating was correct, checking with close friends, relatives, and I did some verifying also with pictures and stories. He even ventured with me on one of my walks. The story was very detail oriented and professionally done. He even got my Grandma to take a photo, which she never does. I was thoroughly impressed with the work he did, as well as the outpouring of support in its release within the Los Angeles Community and beyond. This came just before the release the first book I had ever written, *The Running Miracle*, and I was excited for its coming release.

Here is the story published in the *Los Angeles Times* on February 15, 2017, by Mike Seely:

Reporting from Shoreline, Wash. —
The man runs.
It's damp and just above freezing on a January

morning. He wears shorts and an undershirt and a mesh tank top.

His gait is not smooth or pretty. He has a severe limp, and sometimes he has to walk. His left leg, as he puts it, "is doing all the work."

But he keeps going. Every day for the last decade. Up to 84 miles a week.

Cars honk incessantly, just to say hello. Almost everybody in this sleepy Seattle suburb knows Lamont Thomas, or at least has seen him.

"He'll be out there in the pouring rain with just a basketball jersey," says Sam Wineinger, who works at a car dealership in nearby Everett and started a Facebook page several years ago for locals to discuss the mysterious running man.

Lamont Thomas gets ready for a run. He has become sort of a folk hero in Shoreline, Wash.

"When I made the page, I didn't know his story," Wineinger said. "I can't say I was doing it for the best reasons. If people don't know his story, I can imagine that they'd think he's strange."

The story starts on a March morning in 1989.

Sharron Moore had just dropped off her daughter at work and headed back to northeast Seattle. Her two grandsons, 20-month-old Lamont and his 4-year-old brother, Christopher, rode in back in car seats.

When they arrived home, Moore unfastened their safety belts and walked inside, expecting the boys to follow.

But minutes later it was a distraught neighbor who showed up at the door in a panic. Lamont had chased his brother across a patch of grass and into traffic.

A car had slammed into him, then dragged him four houses down the road.

He arrived at Harborview Medical Center by helicopter in critical condition. Both thigh bones were broken. His skull was shattered. His brain was damaged. His right side was partially paralyzed.

Some doctors thought he might never again walk on his own. One told Moore that her grandson "might be retarded."

Lamont Thomas chats with Kim Vande Griend in Shoreline, Wash., during a run. "You're a great inspiration to a lot of people," she told him.

His childhood was filled with wheelchairs, walkers, crutches and casts. Seizures and bullying marked his adolescence.

"Lamont often forgets to do homework," a special ed teacher wrote on a report card in middle school. "He crumples papers and places them in his backpack rather than his folder. Many times he is sure he has turned an assignment in, but later locates it somewhere in his backpack."

With a damaged right calf muscle and right thigh bone that twists inward, he walked — with assistance — with his feet flaring outward, producing a gait that one doctor described in his notes like this: "He actually has a better running pattern than he does a walking pattern."

It was a prescient assessment.

In his senior year in high school, Thomas began walking on his own. After graduation, he asked his physical therapist about the possibility of running. The therapist expressed skepticism.

So Thomas decided to start running.

"I hated physical therapy with a passion," he said. "I decided that this was my life, this was my game."

Since graduation, he and his grandmother have lived in a two-bedroom apartment in Shoreline, a block off Highway 99.

Most mornings, he catches a bus to the downtown real estate firm where he's worked part time as a clerk since befriending one of the firm's brokers more than a decade ago on a north Seattle basketball court.

He gets home by 2 p.m. at the latest. Then he runs.

He starts on Highway 99 in Shoreline, and heads down a steep hill to the upscale neighborhood of Richmond Beach, perched above Puget Sound. Then he heads back. Each run lasts at least two hours.

"I no longer listen to the pain in my body," he said. "I just go. I just turn my music on and picture somebody across the street trying to race me."

Thomas is not retarded, as a doctor had once worried. Forgetfulness would be the extent of the permanent mental damage that he suffered.

Now 29, he operates the Facebook page Wineinger started and posts inspirational messages to his 2,281 online friends.

"You hold the reigns to your potential!" he wrote recently. "It's often we see visuals of that success and create it as the vision others have obtained. The truth is you are your own story of success so you are in charge of that vision. Never give up!"

Schools and community groups put him onstage to give motivational speeches. With the help of a coauthor, he has also penned a memoir.

He "said to me, 'It'll be really great for me to go and give the talks that I give with this book, because I'll have a script,'" says John Budz, a Seattle resident who cofounded Ward Street Press, which intends to publish the book this year. "He sometimes forgets what he wants to say, and now with the book, he'll have something to read from."

Once a local curiosity, Thomas has become a legend in Shoreline. When he escorts his grandmother to the grocery store, she said, his fans swoon: "There's

*always someone in there who says hey I know you
you're the runner!*

Writing and Publishing

I had a goal in mind of writing a book and getting it published. This process was pretty difficult. Rewriting manuscripts, getting the perfect story together can be pretty daunting, especially trying it on your own without any prior knowledge of the process. The writing part in my case I had down. I had written *The Running Miracle* over the years, starting at age twelve, not knowing it would become an actual book. It was a mess. I had rewritten this story about eight times prior to trying to get in contact with a publisher. When I finally got the opportunity to put it in front of someone, I had a felt I covered everything and made it perfect.

Well, it was perfect in my eyes, but I wasn't looking at it through the eyes of a reader. I could follow it, but for those that had no idea of my life and were just being introduced, let's just say it needed a lot more editing and revision. The hardest part for me was putting it all together in a form in which all would be able to read.

My story wasn't just a story; it was a story about overcoming the near impossible, challenging thoughts and ideas when it comes to telling someone they can or can't do something due to either physical or mental difficulties. It was about maintaining a positive attitude regardless of the difficulties life throws my way, due to the fact the accident happened over twenty years ago.

A lot of facts had to be checked. A lot of the stuff about my injuries I was told about, but due to the substantial trauma my body went through, the memories of those injuries are for the most part unmemorable. But there are events that I recall clearly and these events helped shape who I was becoming. I was running every day after work then coming home and writing. To put everything together, I had to run. It was a habit, and I was trying to make writing a habit too. The stressful part was saving enough time for writing being that it was an inside activity and all I felt like doing was being outside. But I knew I had to make an effort, to sit and write, something I'm really horrible at doing, but I accomplished it over time. Knowing that writing, in a sense, was doing what my running was doing but had the potential of reaching an audience greater than my legs could potentially do.

Running assisted in getting me through some of the toughest times I can recall because of the endorphins. The focus it actually takes for me to get up and do it washes away everything that was going on at the moment. I had both worked extremely hard at staying fit and exercising as well as attempting to get this book released. One special day, Mother's Day, the unthinkable occurred, which would jeopardize my walking, running, writing, and quite possibly my life. A fall occurred, not just any fall, but a break in my left leg. At this point life had come to a complete stop as I found myself in a position I had only imagined happening but its reality had found its way in front of me, and it was in the shape of a parking block.

The Femur Break

—⁓⁓—

It was Mother's Day. I was on my daily run when suddenly, mistiming my step, I tripped over a parking block in the QFC Parking lot in Richmond Beach in front of a Swedish primary care facility, which was closed. At first I was laughing, trying to gather myself as well as to ask "did that just happen"? My cell phone was destroyed by the impact of my 260-pound body falling forward.

At the time all that weight was going knee first into the concrete. I tried to get up, but quickly I realized I wasn't going anywhere. I looked around to see if anyone saw, and no one was around. I was on the ground between two cars, so if a car were to pull into the parking spot I was laying in they wouldn't have seen me. A few people just walked past me; two ladies were just staring. The QFC Manager kept walking, so ultimately I thought I would have to yell for help, which I really didn't want to do.

Finally, I yelled and a person, named Scott Bennett, answered. He asked, "Do you need help?" I answered, "Yeah, call 911." The fire department came, and of course, the Shoreline fire fighters had a joke for me as I was given jokes to them. "We didn't think we were coming to get you; we thought you'd be running," they joked.

At this point, I still was laughing at the fact that this happened. However, the second they moved my right leg I was in so much pain I was ready to fight! I was taken to the emergency room where I was X-rayed. They asked me to move my leg to the side. I said okay. I'm going to tell you right now that the pain I was experiencing was the most pain I think I ever felt outside of surgery. They proceeded to try to take my jeans off without tearing them but couldn't do so without putting me in agonizing pain.

So I said, "Cut them off!" I had never been admitted out of the emergency room to the hospital, so it had to be serious. This is when I began to think of all the things I had to stop doing: work, speaking, being outside, and it started to frustrate me and scare me at the same time. But I remembered this wasn't my first rodeo.

I've never been injured like this before. My right leg has always taken the impacts of my falls. I have never not been able to walk without the assistance of my left leg, it being my dominant leg and all. I often wondered what would happen if I were to lose the ability to use my left side as my right is partially paralyzed. Well, now I would get to experience it first hand, and it's not something I was looking forward to doing. I hated being down and not walking, but having been through this time and time before I developed ways to cope with the fact I might be down for a while.

I wrote a lot before the injury, but I saw myself writing a lot more this time around.

I spent a few days pondering this fact. This was especially difficult because I was thinking far beyond just this surgery. It was a life changer; I thought about running, if I would do it again and if I would be able to gain the strength back to fully use my leg again. This was all cycling through my brain as I lay in a hospital bed potentially facing yet another surgery. Did fear come cross my mind? Yes, but a belief that this would yet become another injury I had to overcome motivated my mindset. The surgeon stopped in to introduce himself along with his assistant. He discussed and explained everything in a way I understood. I was prepared for the surgery but not the reality of it and just how much bone that would be taken from my leg.

Post Injury Realizations

—⟋⟍—

I spent three days in the hospital before the planned surgery. I hated being down and the loss of being able to walk broke my spirit. But I had time to remember before I drifted into full-blown breakdown mode that I've been through this before. In past experiences, I developed ways to cope with the fact I may be down for a while. I spent a few days pondering this notion, wondering how long the I was going to need to recover. But being much older and thinking far beyond just this surgery, I wondered if I would run again by choice? Was it worth the risk? Would I be able to gain the strength back to fully use my leg again? This was all cycling through my brain as I lay in a hospital facing yet another surgery.

My mind was racing in a thousand of different ways; was I going to be in a wheelchair and for how long? I mean, I was ready for whatever the outcome would be? I was a little anxious, wondering when I would get out of this hospital bed? They took me through a hallway to and get me to anesthesia, and I was out. Luckily, I didn't wake up. I've heard horror stories of people waking up in the middle of surgery only to not be heard. This was hard for me to accept because my head and mindset was saying you're going to get through this but the rest of my body was saying you're going to be tied up for a while here and no amount of mind power will change this. Well, the mind is a powerful thing as you will soon find out.

Surgery Day

—⚹—

It was a scary day for me, knowing full well the processes as well as the risk. Only this time the risk was much higher, recovery much more difficult, and having personally no memory of a femur break, I couldn't even think of what they were going to do. It turns out it was going to be a much more complicated surgery because of all my past surgeries. It was far more than just operating on my leg. They had to get through already healed bones, which the surgeon described as a graveyard. It was slated to be a three-hour surgery, but due to not only all the bone but all the other metal in the area, it took another three hours, turning it into a six-hour surgery. I was very surprised when I woke up to find my leg free in the open, which terrified me as well because it allowed me to stretch it and it felt like rubber bands expanding, with spasms of pain rushing up and down my leg. I was just glad I knew why.

The first day was the worst after surgery. It was then that everything played in my head, the timeline of recovery, how I was going to work, when I was going to work, how long it would take until I'd walk again. All these thoughts plagued my mind, and I didn't have a cell phone due to the fall.

When I finally got a grip on things and got a cell phone, I read an email, stating that my book had just been released on Amazon and to the public, and this was exciting news. But I was in no position to celebrate, really just to lay there and smile. It was a pivotal moment in my life and a perfect reason to mentally celebrate. That helped kick-start the mission to overcome yet another adversity.

I spent three more days at the hospital. They wanted to send me home, but feared I would not be able to manage the stairs at my place or at my parent's place. They spoke about sending me to a rehab center for further treatment, but as I thought more and more I concluded that would force me to recover the way another person does, and it wasn't in my best interest. It was then mentioned to me that the University of Washington had an advanced program for those who were strong enough to qualify. I instantly got an adrenalin rush, and in my head the plan was already set. They asked me to move my feet up and down, and move my leg as well. I did it with no problem. I told them this is my dominant leg and it had nothing but muscle in it, and that was easy. They later signed off, and the course was set. I would do the rest of my recovery at the University of Washington.

UW Physical Therapy Rehab

—⚉—

I arrived at the hospital mentally stuck due to the fact I would be potentially placing my all into something different, a therapy for an entire side of my body that had never been tested or had to be used. I instantly got into a mental mode that I achieve only when I'm running and have my head phones on. Endorphins strike my body, pain tries to make itself known, but it doesn't stand a chance. When that happens, it's sort of like a rage of pain comes in and no pains goes out. It's all a mental game. I couldn't believe I was able to finish my rehab there because most people wouldn't even be strong enough or healed enough to do it; it was either here or a nursing facility. I definitely didn't want to be in a facility. I hear it's a much slower process.

Anyway the first day was really difficult speed wise as my mind was in a mode in which my body wasn't healed enough to handle. So I had to literally think before I moved. Not only that, I had a physical therapist holding me with a belt, controlling the speed that I sat and stood. I was frustrated not because I couldn't do it or that I felt like mentally I couldn't, but the fact that I had no control and I couldn't move on my own. That aside, I worked together with the therapist and under my own power and motivation. I wanted to go home, as this was getting irritating.

The therapist was doing her job, wrapping a belt around my waist helping me get up and telling me how to sit down. I didn't like being controlled, and I knew I could walk and sit up and down myself, but I knew she was just doing her job to keep me safe. After just a few more days, I was released to go to my parent's house. This would be a very difficult experience as I felt out of my element and in a place where I didn't feel free to do what I wanted. And the worse part was having to depend on someone else to do almost everything for me. It was hard for me to undertake. I wanted to be in control of something that I had no ability to control.

My Parents' House

—∿∿—

I had thirteen steps at my place and absolutely no way to get up them. Fortunately, my parents, who lived near the Ravenna neighborhood of Seattle, actually had only a steep incline to get into the house. They had stairs too, but having side access made it possible to get in the yard. But I had to conquer the three stairs up front. I got in with no problem.

After that, I realized I would be in this place for an extended period of time. It turned out to be only a month or two, but when you have no idea going in, it can seem like forever. Nevertheless, I was extremely appreciative of the fact I was able to recover outside of the hospital. A trapped feeling started to set in, and I began to think about going outside and what it would take to get there. Having to tell myself to be patient was one of the hardest parts of it. I spent most of that time watching television, eating, and sleeping.

A few weeks later, I started to get up and get things done myself slowly, with a wheelchair by my side. My cautiousness slowly began to fade as my head went straight to overcoming mode, as I began to get tired of not being able to do anything. After time debating, I felt it was time to attempt to go back to Shoreline, to my own space, to my room, and to be able to do things other than just sit. I felt the time was right, but the thirteen stairs I had to climb with just one super weak leg would be one of my greatest challenges from this surgery.

My Right Side and Left Side

—❦—

Most people don't know or can't tell until I say something, but I've been dealing with partial paralysis on my right side since I was young. It requires a lot of the strength on my left side to essentially do the work of two sides. There are often days when the left side just gives out due to overuse, but it still has to hold up everything. It essentially doesn't get a break from the stress, and my right shoe is wrecked on the lower right side within a few weeks.

Unfortunately, this injury was supposed to take me completely out because I wasn't supposed to place any weight on my leg.

Well that didn't happen, and I told the doctors that as well. There would be no other way for me to do anything, no physical therapy, no attempts to walk, no nothing. I wasn't going to let that happen.

Mentally I was already focused on walking again. I still struggle with this today, and this is one of the reasons I had to stop running as you may come to understand in a later chapter. I've had hundreds of right shoes up to this point, and many say I should get a guard made, but what they don't understand is that any change to the motion of my body will cause me to trip a lot easier and cause potentially life altering injuries.

My partial paralysis is on the entire right side of my body, and most of it is filled with fifteen-year-old or longer titanium, which is always great to talk about during speeches, but it is also a real disadvantage when it comes to cold weather. But I have improved in strength, my gait is much better, and strangely, this injury isn't all bad. It kind of evened everything out. My outlook on things has changed a lot with all the new technologies out there, and I'm hopeful with time this will all improve.

Returning Home to Shoreline

—※—

This would be one of the challenges I would come to regret, but also I was more than willing to face. My leg was slowly on its way to healing, but with thirteen stairs staring me in the face, I had second thoughts. Every stair up could be the end of my recovery.

You see I had one leg to do all of this, and it wasn't strong. The railing wasn't sturdy, but I was filled with the same adrenaline I have when I walk or run. I had a determination to finish as I made it to the top. My first thought was get in the house because if I fell or lost my balance the impact wouldn't be as bad, and I was more likely to survive it unhurt. I made it inside and reminded myself once again I had to recover, but my body at this point was ready to go, but I refused to give in. I sat and gave myself a chance to recover with the thought that if I mess up and do something bad, this was my left leg, my dominate one, and I would potentially lose my ability to walk or even worse suffer infection and cause the metal to fail.

After a few weeks, I started walking in short trips to my local coffee shop with my walker. But unlike most, I would push it and I weighed 260 pounds at the time, so the force was wearing on the walker and the back stopper on my walker kept shredding. I wasn't happy and those stoppers weren't cheap. It became a nuisance, but I continued using it until it was just torn through metal and that sound of it scrapping the concrete soon became an annoyance, announcing my presence in the area.

I also used crutches but those too suffered the same fate. It wasn't until I suffered a minor fall that I realized these walks were doing more harm than good. But staying off of it was not possible because I needed to use my left leg to walk, which I will explain later. I slowly did mini laps around my apartment complex, and like past post surgeries, the distances got longer, but this took time and consistency and patience.

The doctors told me it would take up to two years to gain ability to walk again, but past experience has taught me that the words coming from someone who hasn't endured a struggle like mine are simply just words of caution. Defying the odds, I was able to return to walking slowly, and I was back to work in four months. But a lot of this healing and recovery had a lot to do with the fact this was my dominant side and the muscles in my leg were so developed that it really sped up recovery. I also had a bit of an advantage; I was working with a chiropractor previously for my back, and in the middle of our work this injury happened so we switched our focus, and man am I glad we did.

Shoreline Chiropractic

—◊◊◊—

I've been working with Dr. Greg Mack at Shoreline Chiropractic for a little over a year and I'm really picky about who I let work on me. But through the process of dealing with what was a life-altering amount of back pain, it would soon be a thing of the past. Up to this point, the options I was handed for dealing with pain was a needle in the back, which isn't even guaranteed to work. An epidural, yes, the same thing given to relieve pregnancy pain, that would have to happen every six months.

The first time they did it my, L3 L4, and L5 were literally fused together, leaving me hunched over and in stabbing pain. I would use running for adrenaline, and a lot of people asked wouldn't running on it make it worse? My response would always be, "Well I'm not going to sit there and take it. I might as well give it a reason to hurt," since that was the only pain management I had and liked to use.

I've heard positive and negative reviews about chiropractors. My thoughts were that it was just back cracking and bending, and I couldn't do that especially with a partially paralyzed side. I went in to work with Dr. Greg, and unlike the doctors I see that use outdated and unrelated tactics to my very special situation, it was actually explained to me what exactly was being done and I could verify it, not only by the way I felt but the sense it was making.

I was seeing Dr. Greg for my back, but the second I broke my femur, progress wasn't lost but it was a new part I was hoping to build. It was one of the most difficult things to take: the realization that I would no longer be able to run. But I had a new focus, continuing the progress I had made and tirelessly working to get better. Dr. Greg was the first person I actually took knowledge from and applied it. It's been a year and my back pain is gone, and my leg is back stronger than ever. I learned a lot about nerves and how to prevent the pain they cause, and I couldn't be more thankful for the knowledge obtained from this learning process. As of now, I'm a few inches taller, the back pain that was ruining my motivation to make it through was gone, leaving space to place that focus on other passions.

The Running Miracle

—〰—

It was a goal many years ago to just start writing. I wrote lyrics; I wrote poems; I wrote stories, but I always wanted to write a book about myself, about overcoming all the adversities. But it first started when I was in my body cast at the age of ten. I would write to pass the time. I did get depressed a lot, and I was often terrified that I would never walk again. Not being able to go anywhere damaged my mindset.

I was a very happy person, well known in my neighborhood, but I began to notice a change, and I grew more and more angry. I was stressed and very anxious so to tame this emotion temporarily, I would write sometimes for hours. It seemed as if I had endless thoughts when writing, but when it came to talking, I often struggled to find the words to speak. It wasn't until I came across a website in my community about local events and information, I had paid attention to it and followed the page. I thought I could ask if anyone had any information on a publisher in the area, and to my surprise, one person responded. That person is now my editor, Ashley Graham.

I sent her the manuscript of all the writing I did as well as the documentary I did a few years prior. A few days later I got a response from my now publisher, John Budz, at Ward Street Press. Instantly, I was ecstatic just at the opportunity, not thinking I'd hear anything back. I was wrong and a contract was sent. We started working on editing, and I knew it would take some time. My book was due for release in December of the following year, but there were some unfortunate circumstances, and it was delayed. But it was one of the best decisions as it gave more time to do a thorough overview, and before I knew, it was released just after my *Los Angeles Times* interview.

And then I broke my femur, LOL. It was such a rewarding feeling knowing people would get to experience through reading about my struggles and things I've had to overcome to hopefully give them motivation to continue forward. I knew I'd complete it, but I didn't think it would be published. This was truly an attainable dream that took a while to believe.

KING 5 TV, New Day Northwest

—⚏—

I was asked to come to the KING 5 studios for a taping of *New Day Northwest*, hosted by Meg Larson, just prior to my very first book signing for my book, *The Running Miracle* that night at Third Place Books in Lake Forest Park. I was excited for the opportunity to get a bit of exposure. I was a bit shaky due to the camera in my face, trying to ignore it, but the second they started rolling every single ounce of shaky nervousness completely vanished. This usually happens to me prior to any activity involving being in front of people, but this was different. I wasn't alone, and the second I started getting asked questions I was completely chill.

When my mind feels as if I'm forced into a corner, everything in my head that I want to say ignites, and it's completely fluent and put together. It might sound like everything is clear in my mind, but it takes a lot of concentration to just simply talk, but everything worked out. I wasn't safe though; I still had to make it off stage unscathed with crutches and half a working leg, and until I did that, the stress was still on. Luckily it didn't take much; I got through the TV interview, and now I felt ready to conquer my first ever book signing. That confidence lasted for all of five minutes when I finally just said here goes nothing, LOL.

Third Place Books

—⁓—

I had been asked to come do a book signing at Third Place Books, a very well-known bookstore in Lake Forest Park, the same place that was selling my book. I was nervous; I had lots of anxiety not because of the event but the anticipation. My publisher put together a PowerPoint presentation, which relieved some but not all of my stress. It was fear of forgetting and going blank in front of people, which happens a lot more than most simply because processing anything really takes me a lot of time to put things together. It may not seem like it but this has been a struggle since a young age. The majority of the time, I compensated for it by physically showing or trying to describe it in a different way.

You see I was a hands-on learner so reading things and then processing and repeating them was one of my greatest struggles in school, and it even happens sometimes when I speak. I could know exactly what I wanted to say then I would forget, or I would go totally blank and then say something totally not on the subject and it would not make any sense. It was very frustrating and it still is, but I learned to compensate by getting angry not the angry you're probably thinking of, but an anger-driven determined feeling. Suddenly everything comes back, and I can speak coherently speak again without the gaps in what I'm trying to explain.

This exact thing happened at the signing and it was a relief. I spoke for an entire hour and neighbors from my old neighborhood were in attendance. Hazel (my adopted daughter) showed up and totally took over the show. I was still on crutches but managed to lift her. She grabbed the mic with her four-month-old hands and my presentation was over.

College and the Attempt to Remember

—〜〜—

Some of us go straight from high school to college. Some of us go to a two-year junior college and transfer. I learned quite early that college wasn't right for me, but before I came to this conclusion, in high school I received a scholarship from the rotary club for overall excellence. It was $2500 dollars, so I used it to see if I could learn a thing or two. I took law and a business courses at this time, and it was going okay. I felt very comfortable in class, but the moment I left, I remembered nothing, not because I didn't listen, or write down notes and not that I didn't understand, I just didn't remember. It's weird because I would have instances where

I would remember things but couldn't really express it, and then there were times where I went completely blank, as if I wasn't even in the class. Then, at the most inconvenient time, I'd remember when I couldn't apply it. Many people would say, oh well, it happens to everyone or study harder or some other dumb comment, but I continued all the way through to the end of the courses in hopes something would sink in enough to where I could retain it.

My hopes were smashed come test day. It was almost as if I stayed home all semester, stuck in a blind fog. I completely guessed every single question on my test. I was offered more time, but it didn't help it just caused excess anxiety but just because I failed a test didn't mean I didn't learn anything. Forward ahead a few months and an incident happened. If you read my book, The Running Miracle, or saw the documentary, The Man behind the Jersey, you'd know that I was stopped for "jogging while black" by the Shoreline police. They got a call that I was jogging up and down Aurora Avenue North, and they investigated. Mind you, there were two white people directly across the street from me doing the same thing. I instantly remembered everything I learned in law class. I was so angry inside, but I masked it amazingly, calmly just feeding the officer facts about his protocol and ultimately, he just had to leave because he had absolutely nothing on me. It was at that moment I realized I had to get excessively angry or super pumped to remember things, but I also learned that this was a brain injury problem.

Many people say, "Oh well you seem to come across quite fine," and I usually tell them, you're not around me twenty-four hours a day or around me when I'm around my family. It does come and go. It can show up in times of stress and in simply talking if the conversation goes on long enough, but when I am in conversation, I listen and the repetition or pattern of the conversation helps me arrange my words leading to me being able to recover before speaking. I've learned several ways to hide its effects but also to use them in the best way I see fit. Although I did not pass those college courses, I learned a valuable lesson. I can retain things; it's just I learn to apply them differently to expose the true use of them.

Retiring from Running

The day I retired from running was a tough emotional day that turned into a year. I felt I lost my identity and an outlet, as well a piece of myself. In the moments and weeks leading up to and beyond, I felt this loss, but it was a moment to see it from a non-running perspective. In my head I could do anything and I felt like I could still do it, but it was a matter of telling myself it's okay not to run.

This was a moment where I was bombarded with options of riding a bike, or swimming, all great options until you understand my perspective and live the majority of your life in a cast not going anywhere. Riding a bike and having a seizure, then losing control of that bike was too dangerous.

At least with running, I have an option to stop whenever, well almost, LOL.

That's when I reintroduced myself to speed walking. It wasn't just my head and heart taking a hit. What most people don't understand is that walking and running was utilized by me for more than just exercise. I used it when I had a four wheeled walker and wasn't allowed to do the things the other kids would do. I would walk blocks and blocks to prove I was strong enough to do just as or as well as others. I'd use it as a mindset trainer for pain resistance to stay off medication. It was and is a pain killer. It took me a good six months to train my legs to not just take off running. I soon realized that my speed walking was essentially another's running speed. I found people actually have the ability to talk and chat with me when I'm not flying down the street past them, so I've readjusted my purpose to catch up with them (no pun intended), and I'm finally okay with that mentally, physically, and positively.

I focused on the fact I was able to walk again and so that made the transition to speed walking a lot easier. For me, just the ability to exercise carried more weight than most realized, even myself losing the ability to run was like losing an identity. I knew I was much more than just my running, but the repetitiveness of endorphins and good feeling took me away from whatever I was dealing with and that hour or two of calm was one of the best things for me mentally and physically. But realizing I had to give that up felt just that like I was giving up, which I completely am against. But there was a silver lining to all of this. I found a new identity. I didn't feel the need to run, and I would be able to create an even bigger impact without impacting myself or endangering my vision of overcoming and inspiring, and that came in the form of speed walking. As you'll read later, it was one of the best things I could have done for my purpose as I was able to actually connect with those I was trying to reach and inspire.

KOMO News Eric's Heroes

—~w~—

Here is the transcript from my segment on *Eric's Heroes*, which aired on KOMO Channel 4, March 21, 2018 (*https://komone-ws.com/news/erics-heroes/erics-heroes-one-mans-journey-to-continue-forward-one-step-at-a-time*).

"I put music in and I tune everything out," Thomas Lamont said. "But I am aware of my surroundings 24/7." You can tell a lot by the way a person walks. This man's walk is labored. The left foot is pigeon-toed, the right foot drags along the concrete with each step. The body swings to pull that right foot along. "One Saturday I got really bored and I walked up and down here 26 and a half times," Thomas said. It looks like it might be painful, but Thomas walks

nonetheless, with a steady gaze and a sense of a purpose. "Every day that I'm able to use my legs, is a day I'm able to appreciate," he said. "I guess it stems from me not being able to walk... for17 years. Like on and off I've had numerous surgeries and stuff like that put me down. So I'm just trying to make up time, you know? "For many years, the "walking man" was known as the "running man." He could be seen running on the same roads, dragging the same foot, every day. As much as 84 miles a week, which was amazing because he was never supposed to take a single step. "When I was 18 months old, I got hit by a car," Thomas said. "I was told I would never walk again. I had jumped out of my car seat, ran in between two cars, a lady hit me going I don't know how fast. "He had a fractured skull, a broken neck, a shattered pelvis, broken legs, broken arms and a fractured jaw. They thought he'd be in a wheelchair for the rest of his life.

"It got to the point when I was 14 or 15 years old, I revolted. I said, 'You don't know my body. You're not living in this situation; you're not living this way. 'So, I started walking. And then when I was 17, I started walking without the walker," Thomas said. "I started speed walking. I moved here and I started running, and I've been running ever since. "From the beginning, pain has been a constant companion on his journeys. "Basically, I deal with pain on a daily basis," Thomas said. "It's a part of me now. I use it as adrenaline...it's my drug of choice. "Last May, the femur in his left leg, the good one, finally gave out and collapsed.

So now he walks and when he can, he tells his story. "So I couldn't walk, couldn't walk at all," Thomas said. "But, I do have a nice piece of titanium in here now, so every time I walk through the airport it beeps." He tries to help young people understand that the human spirit is an immense, limitless thing. "It's all you. It's all in your hands," he said. "You just need to feed into it and know that you have people backing you and you can do it. Dreams are attainable if you believe."

Thomas works at a real estate firm as a clerk. And when he's done, he embarks on his daily journey. Every day at the halfway point of his walk, he crosses a bridge and arrives at Richmond beach. He admires the scene for a moment, the sun and the water. But only for a moment. "I mean yes, this is beautiful, but hey, I got to get going before my legs decide to say, 'hey, why are we stopped?'" And then the walking man turns around and walks again...toward the future. Toward life on his own terms. Away from an accident and a wheelchair, and pain and fear. Because it is possible to walk toward something and *away from something at the same time. (KOMO 4's Eric Johnson)*

Once this story aired I was completely in shock at the impact. This was the perfect opportunity for me to reach those I would otherwise not have been able to. This interview was a game changer for me as I would just continue forward and grow stronger and regain my ability to walk. I still had a long way to go, but I was well on my way, and I wasn't going down without a fight. I had to continue to strive for my own personal greatness as I encourage others to do as well.

The Power of Extended Family

—ɯ—

Sometimes people have family and an extended small circle. It's been a vital part for me to maintain this for not only my mental health but physical health. There's a common goal to lift each other to do our best and reach the heights of everybody's potential. But in all seriousness, we know each other so well that everyone else around us doesn't quite understand why we are the way that we are. There's no proper way to act and there's always been a trust that whatever we discuss stays there, kind of like "what happens in Vegas stays in Vegas." Jokes aside, when things get rough, it's important to know you have a group outside your blood family to go to with things you don't feel like discussing with family. For me personally, it's been a lifesaver being able to switch the conduct of behavior back and forth and to realize when and where to act, due to my status as well as just being able to not shine a light on it especially being a public figure. It took me so long to get to this point. I was super embarrassed when people would stare at us for being loud or obnoxious or just acting a certain way. It's because of my circle I was able to break that cycle.

We have known each other for years, but who's counting right? They've helped me conquer a lot of fears, and we've been on some adventures most wouldn't have the guts to do. The point I'm trying to make here is that extended family sometimes allows you the space to be yourself and not care about what the world thinks of you, completely tune out the negativity that may be around you and focus on the people in and around you. Sometimes those bonds create a reach to others beyond your own

circle and create a wider circle to extend beyond so that you may welcome new forms
of positive influence. But be aware not all
will add value but most of the time you
and those whom been part of it will notice
and you'll be able to make a group decision instead of just being left on your own.

Mindset and Growing It Positively

—⁓—

I used to channel my everyday pain and adrenaline in a way to make myself feel better. If my legs were giving me pain, I'd go to the doctor and nothing would be done to solve it. This then led me to ignore it, which they tell you not to do. But when you're a special case and nothing is being done to fix it, you do what you can to make yourself comfortable.

I started to think that if I didn't think about it and I stayed active it would go away, and that worked for a little bit, but I then realized I was running a lot more, walking a lot more, and my adrenaline was sky high. I also noticed I was in tons of pain, but I was beginning to then attribute that to the running. The thought of stopping exercising was laughable, knowing it wasn't going to happen, since I felt helpless dealing with the pain signals. I just started to use it as adrenaline as well, which worked well for me. I wasn't going to sit and deal with it; my life was already filled with dealing with it on other people's terms.

I didn't do enough research into where their mindset was, and how they would deal with this. I eventually found my own way of dealing with it: exercise, speaking, and doing something. The mindset that "dreams are attainable if you believe" comes from aspects of my personal life. If I didn't make these things happen with the drive and determination provided from not only myself but others along the way, the process wouldn't have run as smoothly, or at all.

I still use the things I've learned such as pain, adrenaline, and anger to better myself. It's part of my process, and elimination cannot be just done because it too takes a process. Once you understand your processes, you will then be able to better them so that you can grow.

Mind over Pain

—w—

I had two choices: deal with it, or find a way to cope with this pain I was having, which wasn't in one particular place. It was all over and once an area was treated another would flare up, and there was absolutely nothing I could do or the doctors would do. Whether it was because of my age or they just didn't have an answer, but it just became something I handled and still handle. So I took it into my own hands and started rejecting ideas because the majority of them I had already done. Physical therapy was the favorite, and though I hated it, I still gave it a shot until I knew the only person that was going to figure this out was me.

I've been dealing with different issues my whole life, some more challenging than others, but there's been one constant: no drugs. Walking and running were my two drugs of choice. It fed me adrenaline, and I could exercise to the point where I felt that pain was reasonable or I felt the full effects of an adrenaline rush.

In the past, I've been asked when I do that doesn't it make it worse? I look at them and simply say, when you use your pain and transfer it to push you harder, it no longer becomes an issue. It will return, but for the moment the only thing that matters is that I finish walking or running or exercising. I'm talking about a curved spine that sends pain up and down my back, arthritis mixed with it, and one side of my body holding eighty percent of my weight. But even with all that, running sends a rush of determination throughout my body.

The anger I had with the thought of attempting to be stopped is turned around, all the while remembering that I'm about to do something many doubted. I take off, running off the negative energies thrown at me throughout the day. Exercise has been my outlet for so many things; it has also brought me to being in a position of inspiration for others, and pushing me further towards speaking. In the back of my head, the thought of not being in a position to simply walk almost happened again for the eighth time. Having your ability to walk taken away but still having the thought process to say "oh really, well see about that" begins to take a toll if you're not ready to initiate your mindset.

Raising of a Child that Isn't Yours

—∽—

Hazel came into this world in December, approximately four months prior to me breaking my femur. She was everything I expected a kid to be, limitless, an expert climber, and crawler extraordinaire. Her father wasn't present, so I was the main male figure she'd see, and I was cool with that.

I figured I could give her a little balance. I knew I wasn't her father and that was something as she grew older I could explain, but in the meantime I figured I'd provide structure for what was to come. But unfortunately right before she turned five months old, I suffered my femur break. It was a devastating blow and not soon after as I was awaiting surgery she stopped by with her mother and she was her same old self, but calm until she spotted the lift bar above the bed. She kept climbing to try to reach it, staring at it as if it were a new toy. I then proceeded to lift her. She reached for the bar and wouldn't let it go. It looked like she was dunking on a hoop, getting air time.

She started touching, investigating, crawling, and wreaking havoc on anything in her sight. She took away a lot of the worry about my injury because my focus was on keeping her safe, ha-ha. I eventually got my ability to walk back, and when I did she was only months behind me, so I got lucky. I treated her like my own, knowing she wasn't, I still wanted to keep a sense of normalcy in her life. I still remember when she put her first "Da Da" together. It just happened. It happened again and again, but we just treated it as her talking because I wasn't sure, but as she started talking more and more it became clearer. Luckily she heard my name and I asked her could she say it? She goes

"Mont!" I'm like, I'm cool with that. Better than the alternative, LOL.

It's not that I didn't want her to call me dad. I just wasn't, and I wanted to get that out of her system early. She's been through a lot, and now she's only two and has progressed so much since the time she was born. A walking talking two-year-old who is always testing the boundaries of my running skills.

It was awkward in the beginning for me because people saw me with her so much word started to spread that I had a daughter. I just let it be; I really didn't care my because my priority was making sure she was safe and taken care of. I had a similar experience growing up, only I had people all around me so the thought of a father not being around never bothered me. I wanted to make it so she had a constant male figure to fill the gap if one was there.

It's not important to me to have a title, but that she's reassured. I didn't grow an attachment, but I learned what it was like to put all your effort into caring for one child. It's hard, stressful at times but it was rewarding for me and I knew the impact I had and still have without being forced. It's true when they say a kid changes your life, you got to grow up quicker, pay attention when your half-asleep, and have your childhood energy, which started disappearing when I was twenty-five, but I kept pace with her. Here is the kicker. I stepped up and helped take care of a child that wasn't mine, and I'd like to point out she is white. Many points and stares were made when I would walk down the grocery isle with her, but it didn't faze me. I also knew I was proving a point; anyone can step up or step out, and at the end of the day I knew I was doing the right thing and it is what she deserved. She doesn't know how much she helped me just by being herself.

PTSD *and Anxiety*

—⟋⟍—

Unfortunately, PTSD and anxiety are way to common. I myself have them but for reasons most haven't experienced. It's something one just can't get over, but manage. Luckily for me, I've trained myself to use walking and running as a deterrent.

My personal battle with PTSD stems from all the years of surgeries and anxiety of when or if I'll walk again. Mind you, I've been put in that position over five times, some due to injury some due to surgery, but it's all the same from the time the surgery is planned until its completed then on to healing time to just sitting around. I've been stuck in multiple body casts multiple times, and it wasn't fun, nor do I wish it upon anyone. So every day that I can go for a walk is a privilege because I know how it is not to be able to walk. Safety reasons, that feeling of being stuck not being able to physically do anything for months has haunted me for years. Just going through it and the way my body is I'm always aware of it and try my best enjoy the time I have. What's weird is I do get anxiety going on stage, but it lasts just up until the event. Once it's Showtime, that's when I begin to come out of it because it's at that point that I know there's no turning back.

It's kind of like an endorphin high if you will; the sooner you start the sooner you finish. The funny thing is most people have no idea what's going on inside of me. Facial reactions never show it. Big crowds are a trigger; I've got to know where the exit is but I'm sure many others do too. Also, when my next surgery may have to be is an anxiety trigger. I had a scare a year after femur surgery because it wasn't healing correctly, but those worries went away as I got bigger and stronger. With so much bone loss due to the surgery, they claimed that they may have to inject me with a steroid, but that involved taking everything out. I wasn't excited at all. I had done all that work and they were trying to take me down again, so I said naw, I'm cool, will deal. The anxiety still grew because what they stated was you'll know if the parts fail; the hip will collapse. I had to move on and just do my own thing. I soon learned to differentiate the pain from my healing femur and the pain from the rest of my body as the femur improved. Eventually, the anxiety from the femur dissipated, and I continued on.

The Limp

I have had this for years. One side sways to the other, and it's because one side is completely smaller and shorter than the other. This causes my body to sway and causes severe pain, and it's one of the main reasons I had to get my hip repaired at such a young age. It was taking all the weight from my right side and causing a severe impact with every step I took, so as I was recovering from surgery I couldn't tell which pain was which. All I knew was it hurt, but my body hurt all the time, so I just dealt with it.

No doctor really listened and they just told me to do PT, which if you read, The Running Miracle, you'd know my feeling on that. I've had my share of people staring as well, and now my feelings on that are if you're going to stare at me, and you're a grown ass person, then don't get mad if I stare you down. I've learned most are looking for the reason why I was limping, and they are too afraid to ask and think staring is better. I used to have a problem with this, but if it's going to happen it's going to happen and I get to laugh when I say "WHAT!"

My limp has also gotten me a lot of positive attention, and I've been able to turn it into inspiration for myself and the people around me. Since I had femur surgery, now the left side is shorter than the right, but Dr. Greg and I, who I mentioned before, pointed me towards a custom-made lift, and it evened everything out. Unfortunately, I still had the shoe dragging issue on just the right side so the upper corner of my right shoes are destroyed (sometimes every month sometimes sooner), but I'm more aware of it and can catch it. But if my right leg is struggling when I'm walking, there isn't very much I can do about it. Since I've stopped running, the length of time my right shoe has lasted has extended greatly though I do miss it. I've saved hundreds of dollars on right shoes and my gait, which was once completely curved, is straight and aligned. It took a lot of patience to finally have a painless back that didn't look like a snake on the x-ray machine, and I'm a few inches taller as well. This has been a twenty-five-year mission to get rid of, and now it's taken care of in less than two years. It's a miracle what your body can naturally do for you when you allow it time to not only heal but feed it what it needs.

Transitioning to Speed Walking

---✦---

I see walking as a privilege. After losing my abilities more than just a couple times, it's something I must do even if I'm tired, sore, or just mentally not there. The thought in my head is when is the next surgery? When is my hip going to give out? That mixed with the emotions of having to give up voluntarily a passion of doing something as simple as running for walking took a while to get used to, both mentally and physically.

I knew I could still take off, no problem, but whether my leg would break again or not was another story. Knowing that my mind and body don't get along, just like my left and right leg are a team until I get competitive then it's over. But I knew for the longevity of both my body, I had to find a middle ground for running that both took care of my physical wants, feeling-wise and keeping my body fit.

A lot of people tossed the word 'gym' in the mix, but I won't do gyms. It's something I've tried quite a few times, and it's just not something for me. Swimming has also been suggested, and to be honest I was forced to do that for physical therapy and had no interest in it. No offense, but when you're forced to do something for so many years, it takes a mental toll on you or at least it did on me. Yes, it's good for you, but I want to do something I actually enjoy, and swimming for excise purposes isn't one of them.

So I found a way to bridge the gap between running and getting the same adrenaline that I get from running from speed walking. And, it actually works with less impact. I actually feel as if I'm running, and it burns a lot more for me. I'm also able to stop and talk, unlike before where I'd fly past people. It's a good change and also fills the gaps that I would have lost all together, and the best part is my right shoes don't suffer as much damage and last a lot longer.

Becoming a Public Figure

—⁓—

Moving to Shoreline, many people didn't know me or who I was or what I was doing walking so much. Eventually word got around and few newspaper articles later, I was known and a Facebook page was created by a local kid describing the random guy who walks in jerseys in Richmond Beach. Because everyone saw me but no one knew my name or bothered to ask, people would say you know there's a page on Facebook about you? Of course, I thought they were kidding, but I came across it about a year later and just kept reading speculation about whether I knew about this page.

Well, I finally answered that question after I posted on it for the first time and nothing but positive nice messages were on the page. I finally decided to ask the creator to allow me to take it over, and I did this in 2010. That was the time I started creating posts to inspire others, and that came with responsibility. I knew my impact would only grow as would my visibility, which was not a problem for me. I maintained the same attitude off-screen as I did on-screen; I would go outside and hear honks and screams, "you're that guy"! Multiple times a day it made me smile knowing I had such an impact because the pain I was in was more than most could possibly handle, but being used to it I smiled and went along with my day.

It wasn't hard to be positive because I knew what it's like to not be able, and that was one of my main motivators. The others came from the people I inspire because I knew the pain I was in wasn't for nothing. But it goes even further than that; you must be who you are at all times out of respect for those who know you because of public personality. I'm no better than I was prior to the attention. However, I've been getting more aware of who is watching me and what I'm doing to better those around me.

Battling with a Body that Wants to Quit

—⟋⟍⟍⟍—

There have been times when my body has either temporarily quit on me or wanted to quit. I had arthritis pain with every step, which is an everyday thing from the moment I start my day until I go to sleep. Sometimes it even comes in the middle of exercise, but I know the difference between overdoing it and just pain. I learned very early on to battle it, and it does get tiring, but usually exercise strategies to fight it have been one of the greatest remedies for it. Thankfully now it's no longer a back problem, but it's simply nerves, and I have an idea of what causes it and healing it through exercise and music are critical when it comes to mental healing.

It revitalizes my mindset to be able to find a way to stop the pain. It'll be there, but I will be smiling, laughing, and ignoring it for as long as I can. This is a method I had to use due to the fact of being told over and over again that they can't fix it other than with a shot in the back every six months or back surgery, which they said could make it worse. I wasn't going to do either originally but it got so bad I said you know, let's try the needle.

By this point I was in so much pain my lower back felt like it was folded in half, so I just decided to give it a try. The problem was the needle was huge, and I kept looking at it like how you going to put that in my back, thinking are you going to numb me or something. I got a response that the needle will do that already. Suspicious, I turn around thinking it's going to be a quick poke. I was so wrong. They told me it'll take like five minutes. The very second the needle touch my nerve, I lost it and told the doctor take the needle out now!!!! I was not having it; I'd been in a lot of pain but that tops it. I then proceeded to see a back specialist and he said physical therapy and I just left. I don't know exactly what was wrong, and I had a good feeling it wouldn't be figured out. I had been sent around in a circle of doctors, and I wasn't doing it again. I found that I needed to find alternative methods. I had to do something to offset the negative effects of it as it was affecting me.

Returning to Work

Immediately after my fall my mind went straight to how long will it take me to walk again. When will I work again? These questions were circling my thoughts to the point where I became enraged, and when I become I angry my adrenalin usually takes over and every bit of pain disappears. Knowing that the repercussions of falling could potentially kill me or further the injury and potentially cause a loss of my leg, I was extremely careful about the timing of my return to work. Luckily, instead of being out of the office six month to a year, I was able to make it back in just four months.

The overuse of my left leg sped up the healing time of the injury dramatically. It was incredibly hard to tell myself to slow down due to my mindset and being in this position in the past. My first visit back at work I was in a wheelchair, so I had a friend drive me, and I brought Hazel with me. You'll hear more about her later. I went in August with plans to start in December; it was good to be back in the office after being so patient mentally not pushing myself to get back. That was my new motivation not that I didn't have enough already.

A month flew by seriously fast and before I knew it September came. My mind was racing as it was the night before I decide to return, nervous was an understatement as I was thinking about getting on the bus with crutches and getting off with them as well as getting there and getting home, but like most things it was completely fine. Eventually, I was able to walk without the crutches and it made getting to work and moving around so much better and not so painful. I still had to use the crutches for long distances, but work wasn't one of them.

Music and the Hill

—ɷ—

My day usually started out running up and down Richmond Beach not one hill not two but three and sometimes even going to the Edmonds ferry dock. But you see it wasn't just walking to me; it was a challenge. It looks like the same hill, but I always change one thing to make it more challenging whether it be a faster speed or a slower walk, even different breathing techniques. There was always something new with each walk, sometimes the purpose behind it would change. Sometimes it was just for me thinking about the meaning of why I'm out there. Other times just exercise.

The music helps to tune myself out and focus; it all depends on how I'm feeling. What I'm going to listen to if I'm in pain is probably some hip hop and a lot of the time I am in pain when I start but eventually the music mixed with the endorphin high causes the pain to completely disappear. There is a mental recovery time as well. I'm actually doing something productive and not sitting which makes me feel even more driven to do it.

There are times where the pain is so bad that I ask myself just what the hell I'm doing, but I've been dealing with it for so long and what I was told to do to relieve it never worked. I had to find a way to mentally deal with the fact that the pain wasn't going away otherwise, and so I started using running and walking as a way to manage the pain. It was something I was told I'd never do, so every time I did it and completed the hill, I knew I was not only proving wrong all others who I said I couldn't do it but also giving myself the high that comes with completing something you said you would. That was one of the many reasons I continued to do it regardless of the stabbing pain and arthritis that hit with each step, and the roller coaster of pain running up and down my back, and that was something I promised myself wouldn't stop me. I would just push through until I made it to the top. The second I sat down all the nerves relaxed and about an hour later I was ready to do it all over again.

I remember it was a Saturday. I had nothing planned I decided I'd see just how many times I could walk up and down 185th Street to the beach, either until I physically couldn't or I got fed up with the scenery. Well, seven times and about 1000 stairs later, I finally gave myself permission to stop. I knew I could do more, but I had to give myself time to recover.

The Word "Disability"

—*◊◊◊*—

A lot of people refer to the word disability, whether it is mental, physical, or something else, which doesn't define me in any way. I averaged more miles than a person with two good legs at eighty-four miles a week. The excruciating arthritis pain up and down my body continued, but my vision of overcoming it stayed front and center. I learn in a different way than most people, sometimes recalling information at a later time when it's not necessary. Many times I'm in mid-conversation and something to do with that subject comes up much later in another conversation, causing it not to make sense but that's the way my memory works.

I had a test done by a doctor and the proof came after that. The doctor would tell me a story with specific things to remember, and after asking me a specific question about the story, I could not retain it and my mind went blank. It caused massive frustration because I wanted to remember everything, but I couldn't. It was also a positive because I found out what was wrong and I could potentially address it. Still, I continued on with learning, figuring out which learning style worked best for me, and I learned that if I get enraged or upset, I would retain most things. Take law class. I failed twice, but I seem to retain it. When others need my opinion or help understanding something, I myself don't learn without having to apply what it is you're teaching me, and for some reason it works for me.

I know I'm smart, and I know I can do things most people think I can't. I've had people judge me, and I've had people assume I couldn't do something simply based off of my walking. But what most fail to realize is some of us perform a lot better than some assume. I realized I was different at an early age and that was one of the most powerful things because the negative, mean, and judgmental things people have said only reflect their inability to have a wider view of what's in front of them. Most of the time they become embarrassed by just how powerful or comfortable you are in your own shoes. I'm prepared to realize that I'm not the same. I really don't want to be, and I have my own advantages and disadvantages, but the power of my mindset takes those disadvantages and creates positive visions for them. Sometimes you can become your own enemy due to your inability to tune the negatives out. I struggled with this for years until I found just how much I had overcome.

The Femur Repair

—॥॥—

I continued to see Dr. Greg, but as I did in previous surgeries, I made my own regimen of getting my strength back. No gym, no hardcore work out, just simple walking and stretching. I was 260 pounds at the time so weight wasn't in my favor either. I was so focused on my femur, and I knew how determined I was. It was scary, I had to be super cautious everywhere I went and worry about every ache and pain and the most serious infection. I couldn't stop thinking about how bad I was going to crush the expectation of everyone. Running was an emotional outlet that was taken away from me, and I wasn't happy about it. That was my pain management, emotional support, my mental drive, and my inspiration to myself and others.

I worked tirelessly to get back to my ultimate self, but to understand that struggle you first have to realize that I was doing all of this on my one leg that I broke and that I could easily break again just from supporting my weight. That was a risk I was willing to take. Dr. Greg started loosening the nerves in my femur all while simultaneously working on my back. The doctors were telling me constantly to slow down, but I couldn't listen to them because they hadn't been through this challenge nor the challenges before this.

In high school I had to get surgery in November of my senior year, knowing full well that I had to complete my senior project. But with two inches of bone left in my hip, I had to get it done. I had the option to skip my senior project all together, but I felt sitting around for three more months wasn't right, and I wanted to contribute to the class, so I accepted the challenge. After surgery, the recovery timeline was about two years. I continued my efforts and smashed the timeline to just under nine months. In this case, with the assistance of Dr. Greg, we completely changed the game. My mindset was in total drive mode, and there was nothing stopping me other than the thoughts of injury, which I continued to laugh at.

We got to a point where I felt absolutely no nerve pain, no back pain, none. Of course, it returned if I over-worked it, but that's normal. My left leg got to the point where I could return to running, but I stuck to the very safe and less impactful speed walking. I didn't want to lose my ability to walk or the use of my left leg permanently. I found it to be more inspiring and impactful, and I continue to do it to this day.

The Return to Richmond Beach Road

—⚏—

Fresh off retiring from running, I decided I would maintain my athletic activities, only now I was at a slight disadvantage. I had a new leg still healing from surgery, an unsupported right leg, and a slightly shot mindset, simply because of the two-month scare of potential surgery. I had to regain that mind power and go for it. I hit the hill with the walking speed of a runner, thinking of all that transpired. Adrenaline hit anger and in an instant a running-like high hit my body, which was sending pain signals constantly, but I tuned those out because I knew the difference between regular pain and "you better stop before I stop for you pain." A lot of people don't know that the pain never stops because were dealing with more than just one area. It's like a spotlight, but when I exercise, I get in the mindset of "you want to hurt, I'm going to give you a reason to hurt," but I was still stuck because I had to learn how not to run. What I mean is when my body, especially my legs, start speed walking, it usually progresses to running as soon as the pain hits. Or there is a person jogging across the street, and my leg begins to think we're going to race so I take off.

I had to do that hill in sections, knowing I'd eventually get to the bottom. I didn't stop, though I constantly thought about finishing and getting to the bottom simply to prove mentally I could get there. It was a hard realization to figure out. I couldn't do it the same, run down the stairs or even jump, but I also realized if I listened to the people trying to control my physical activities, I potentially wouldn't have gotten there at least in the time I did. I went a step further; I took my travels to Edmonds ferry dock, but

I'm going to tell you I've never struggled so much to actually get there. I went the long way though.

This is what happens when you're so driven to prove to yourself and to everyone else you're not the same, you're not like everyone else, and you don't need to be. I got there, and it took a significant amount of time, but I made it there and back. I got to the water and sat there thinking of all the people who didn't even think I had a chance and laughed. I also set my goals higher. I had been keeping them low based upon a potential surgery, but it was time for bigger and better things.

Being Cast in a Movie

I had been going to this particular coffee shop for years where I met two brothers. I'd see them sometimes on the road running, sometimes at the coffee shop, and as we progressed talking I told them my story and they were shocked. I saw them a few more times, and I heard rumors that they were going to get me in a movie. I was enthused at the idea, but wasn't sure that anything would come of it. But stranger things have happened.

Eventually, I got an email with a script. The plot was two big-city teenage sisters are sent to their grandparents' farm for Christmas break against their wishes. While there, the sisters connect with their roots and help save the farm from foreclosure. I would play a horse caretaker named Reggie. I instantly thought to myself, "this can't be real." Well it was, and they were going to film a week from the time I got the script. After the happy freak-out, I was anxious, asking myself how will I remember this. It was two pages long!

Determined I tried and I tried for four days, but like speaking engagements, the way I deal with it is once you're up there, you're on. But I was constantly told it's a relaxed atmosphere and it's a just a get together; you'll be cool, and it was, eventually. I still was looking at the script when we got up there, and I got to look at the other actors and actresses do their parts, not knowing when they would call me for mine. When the time to shoot my scene came, my insides were going to explode. It was that day I realized I hated cameras or at least being in front of them.

With the other actors needing to do other scenes, you couldn't tell I was freaking out. I tried to follow the script, and I struggled a little, but I got a lot of it and at the end I just freestyled, and it was perfect.

After a lot of editing, they really spotlighted my positive presence, and for acting in front of the camera I feel as if I did a pretty good job, anxiety aside. A few months go by and I get a call. It was a Sunday, and the person asked if I would like to attend a red carpet event for the movie. I jumped at the opportunity, not sure if I was ready to see myself on a big screen, but I was excited for the opportunity nonetheless. I had my good friend Daniel with me. I was interviewed, I got to take a few photos and watch the film. When I saw myself on screen I still couldn't believe it. I finally got to accomplish something I had been thinking about for some time, and I could knock it off my bucket list.

Epilepsy

B ecause of a closed head injury and brain injury, I've have had episodes with seizures, sometimes with some warning and sometimes they just happen. For those who don't know, my seizures come on randomly, and in some instances I have enough warning to get to a safe place. But even if I'm in a safe place and I have one, I'm not always safe, and unfortunately my coworkers were witness to one of my really bad ones. I had no warning, and I ended up splitting my head open in the back room and suffering a double concussion.

Now comes the part where a lot of people don't follow. I when I wake up from a seizure, I have no idea who you are, where I am, and how I got there. So fight or flight instinct is initiated, and I will fight you if you hold me down, and if your fingers are placed incorrectly, they'll get bitten off. That applies for any person having a seizure, so if your trying to keep someone from swallowing their tongue, keep your hands away from the mouth. They say you not supposed to hold a person down after a seizure. Well that's probably why. Anyway that was just the worst one, and if you're wondering, knock on wood, I haven't had one for about three years. I share the info personally because I hear a lot of confusion about what to do after. Having a closed head injury along with brain trauma keeps me susceptible to these, and knowing this, the majority of my friends and family know what to do.

I choose not to drive because there is the potential to have an episode. I'm not going to put others' lives in danger for a luxury I could potentially do without. Epilepsy has many forms. Some people have it, and you wouldn't even notice, no shakes, no sudden movement, or anything. They are more common than you think. Sometimes the reasons for not sharing range from a simple fear all the way down the line to discrimination or being treated differently, so I'm sharing what I know about my personal battle with it.

Las Vegas and the NBA All-Star Game

—〰—

Prior to becoming a public figure and getting my name out there, I met a guy named Zaid. I was walking around Shoreline Community College, on one of my trips around Shoreline, and I told him my story and he was amazed by my efforts not to give up. We talked a few more times after that and had become really good friends. He was in the midst of completing his novel, Darkness to Sunlight, a story about his life and career in the NBA. It's a great read. After it was completed, I found out I was featured in a chapter of his book. It was the first time ever that I had my story in some other publication. While talking, he stated he was going to Las

Vegas for a book signing at the NBA all-star game, and he had ask me to come and help with it.

I had been to Vegas a few times but never around the time of any big event, let alone an all-star game. I still wasn't used to that kind of heat, but I figured I could handle it. The flight down was okay, but for the guy three seats over, 6-foot-9 NBA power forward and center Don Smith, I could only imagine. I'm 6-foot-3 and it was a tight squeeze for me. I'm extremely afraid of heights and guess who had the window seat! Even though it was only a two-hour flight, it felt longer, maybe my anxiety was secretly adding time. I do fly a lot, but I'm freaked out until we get it the air, the climbing of elevation if you will. We were invited to a legends meeting where some of the greats would get together and watch the game together. I had no idea who would be there, and as I was walking through the hotel, Larry Bird walks right past me. I'm in bitter shock as he was so much taller than me. I continued to the back room, and I had no idea who would be there at the meeting.

I entered and sat down, and I see Downtown Fred Brown, along with Clyde the Glide Drexler, as well as Slick Watts, all of whom were very nice people and very approachable. I even came across Kareem Abdul-Jabbar. It was interesting because at that moment I wasn't star struck or looking for an autograph or anything. I was just talking to them as if they were just ordinary people. While talking to them my head was just thinking about the illustrious careers they had and where and what they are doing now. I feel it's important for them to show the youth and the people who follow your life after basketball and allow them to see that basketball is only part of the what you do and not who you are.

Public Speaking

—ɯɯ—

I love people, especially speaking to them about my life, my challenges, and what I've overcome. The difficulty comes when I hit the stage. It's not the people but the pattern I go in, not every speech is the same. I have to tell the story of my journey several different ways, but eventually it all comes to the same inspiring point. Many ideas hit my head when I start speaking to the point where my anxiety kicks up and everything goes blank. Parts of the story I was originally going to tell simply fly off as if they weren't even there. It's fun but it's also very irritating at times to test myself. My publisher put a PowerPoint together for me. It was organized precise and simple, and he thought it might help with memory organization, but what happened was I was constantly staring at the screen and the moment I looked away everything when blank.

The same thing happens with tests but what happens when I get enraged when I can't remember is that suddenly everything comes back. Whereas if someone else has an issue, I usually have the correct answer for them and can assist but not so much for myself. So, when I speak, the same thing happens, and only if someone asks a question, I can answer it and it usually helps and everything starts to comeback. Its challenging, but I get the result I need to complete the speaking opportunity I seek.

260 to 200

T wo hundred and sixty pounds was the heaviest I had ever been, but it took my femur breaking to really get out of hand. To some this may not seem like a big jump, but I was in a position where the leg that had all the muscle to support me was broken, so I literally could do nothing weight-bearing, like go on a running spree or lift or anything like that. I had to wait until I got the go ahead mentally and physically from my body to just let loose.

The process was challenging at first because I was still regaining the ability to walk, trying to see if I had the strength to not only handle all the weight but also the sway of my body throwing extra weight at it. I will tell you, it took several months of trial and error, feeling pain I shouldn't be feeling, scared out of my mind, until finally I just said you know if something is going to break let it. I had to get moving, so slowly I got back to walking.

It was one of the most mind numbing things to walk because I knew I could run. I had a feeling I could actually shed the weight faster. Three years prior to the femur break, I was a solid 185. Prior to the break, I was touching 225 so my focus became to not only walk but to lose all the excess weight. I didn't change a thing as far as eating, but I did take my walking to another level. I also changed my speed and the calories, and the weight started dropping. I didn't want to follow somebody else's plan because I know what works for my body, and if it didn't, I'd eventually find a way to make it work.

My body wasn't meant for all these workouts. Hell, my body wasn't made for my mindset, but I'd been sitting more than I wanted, and this femur wasn't supposed to be fully healed for two years. But I tweaked that timeline just a little, and as of now I'm at 210 pounds, and my femur is healing and continues to heal daily.

Striving for Ultimate Greatness

—ᘉᘉ—

I have a saying. I try to live by striving for ultimate greatness. A lot of people wonder about the meaning behind it, so allow me to explain. There have been many times and many incidents where all my strength, my attitude, my mindset, and my body has been challenged. If not for the connection of all those elements, I have a firm belief that I would not be in the position of power I'm currently in. It has been challenging for me on multiple occasions to shake the thoughts of others on either my progression or the way I handle my post injury healing. But when I finally realized the power I had to change the minds of those who brought this information to my attention, I looked at them like they were crazy.

My body is unlike most. The healing time, the athleticism, the pain level, and my mindset are factors to deal with it. You're in full control of the attitude you bring to any situation. You may not be in control what happens to you, but you are in control of the mindset you carry moving forward. I have no idea what someone else is going through. I can only trust my own process and hope it brings a light to those lost in darkness as they attempt to overcome adversities placed before them. The phrase, striving for ultimate greatness, I feel, embodies the actions I hope you have the courage to follow.

The Right and the Left Leg

——⟋⟍——

Many of us have differences in our body as far as length and strength on one side or the other. In my case there is a major difference. An inch and a half may not seem like a lot, but it can have a major effect on your body as a whole. My right leg and left leg don't interact well due to my brain injury. It makes it super difficult to balance, which affects how my body functions. It got so bad that my hip had to get repaired because it was shaving the bone all the way off of the hip joint itself.

It doesn't stop there. Even my arms are a different length. When I would run my gait would slide to the left and there would be nothing there. My right foot would trip over the left and still occasionally it does, but these adversities I'm thankful for because it's given me a deep appreciation for my abilities. But it does take a monthly toll on my shoe. Yes, I said shoe because while my left shoe is shiny and beautiful, the bottom left corner of my right shoe is heavily damaged due to weakness and dragging or the right foot attempting to catch up to the left foot. I later figured out that a potential lift could be made to offset the difference, so one was created and fortunately it worked!

It took several months and many adjustments for my body to simply adjust to the sudden change, but in the end it helped me become pain free in my back as all the pressure slowly left and I was able to stand straight and the curve in my spin disappeared. My body is still adjusting two years after my femur break, but on the whole, the pain is now manageable as I work to become pain free throughout my whole body.

Sports and Performance

〜〜〜

I love basketball. I'm the assist guy that had a hook shot. When I'm playing my focus was solely on defense and passing. I would occasionally shoot, but I loved to drive the lane with a layup. The problem came when I couldn't switch hands; it was always the left with the occasional right.

When it came to football, I was a quarterback due to the fact I had so much metal in my body. If I were to take a hit it probably would be my last. My balance was terrible, but it was also an advantage because I was fast. My agility was there, and I was also very tall and could throw the ball high. I focused on what I could do and used those talents to compensate for the things I was in the process of learning.

I come from a family of athletes, so I've watched over many years and learned visually what works and what doesn't work. I've tried to apply those consistently with the body I had. I was a runner, so speed was an advantage with every sport I played, but with that there were a ton of injuries, like shin splints and twisted ankles due to the overlapping of my feet tripping each other. The thing I had to remember was I was picked to play something when I was younger. I didn't have the opportunity to do some things simply because of my abilities, and also having a walker so that thought along with the fact that I was playing gave me a sense of comfort. I did what the doctors said I'd never do, and I am performing better than they claimed. It goes to show you what a strong mindset and an unstoppable drive can do when you are attempting to overcome the impossible in the eyes of so many before you. You oversee the process of how far you decide to challenge what others say is impossible.

The Can't Mentality

—⁓—

Many times I've heard this term, whether its towards me or someone else. The doctors I've seen used to love this term until I completely demolished their thinking. The truth was I could do anything, but to their standards, I couldn't or I was not permitted to or not healed enough or to weak which I found incredibly funny. They had no idea until recently just how powerful my mindset and mentality had become. For example, after my femur surgery, I can do almost every activity I did prior to surgery and injury, but this was supposed to take three years. I understood it is common practice to not get one's hopes up, but if not for my stubbornness I'd probably be where they assumed I'd be. Living on someone else's timeline isn't always the smartest move because they don't know what your capabilities are. Your strategy to overcome is the one thing, if not the only thing, to stop you from your own progression, or at least that was true in my case.

From the basketball court, kickball, football, soccer, we all have slightly different abilities. Sometimes you're better than others and sometimes that kid you see as weak or can't play may play better than you think. Your vision of someone else's skills will bite you in the end, so beware, your eyes can indeed fool you if you're not mentally prepared to handle what you see.

Many times I've walked into a physician's office and I've heard the most negative of negative comments as to my prognosis. Most say that's what pushed me and that couldn't be farther from the truth. It did cause constant worry, fear, the feeling of wanting to give up, and sadness, so I ask you to take a moment if you're in a position to do so. Physicians, give your diagnosis, but after, give the patient confidence that you will do all you can to help them beat it, whatever they're are going through. Simple words like that can make or break someone.

Arthritis

—⚬—

Arthritis is something I've been dealing with since I was young, although most look at it as something you get when you age. For me, first it was from my back and being slouched over like a black hunchback up a until high school through no fault of my own. I just wasn't able to stand up straight. Multiple surgeries didn't help either, four of which left me in a body cast or spika cast. The cast actually was meant to wrap around my body, but the unfortunate part was it was affecting my back. I could only lay on my back, placing undue pressure on my back for a grueling eight weeks to sometimes as long as a year. Depending on the surgery, my body was already weak from the accident so it made it a lot easier for arthritis to appear after every single surgery. It was already present so of course it's going flock to a newly worked on area.

Winters really sucked for me because it didn't matter if I was inside or outside, I would feel that cold air coming and cold air for me equaled severe pain. Medication like ibuprofen helped a little but overall, I was going to deal with it because I was used to it. Eventually arthritis traveled from my back to my new femur to my knees and so on. I have it currently and the majority of the time arthritis is the cause of most of the pain, but what the arthritis doesn't understand is pain is just another reason for me to push harder.

Many say listen to your body, and I fully agree with that unless you've been dealing with something like this for years and know how to handle it appropriately. Other people's approaches to my struggle often fall short of my personal expectation, so I keep the battle to myself.

Long Distance

I'm told that I'm seen walking all over the place in Seattle, Edmonds, Mountlake Terrence, Lynnwood, and so on. I like my distance walking because it allows me to release all the negatives that are impacting me at the moment. It's my happy place if you will; the adrenaline alone is enough to do it for me.

Many look at me like I'm crazy when I tell them about the journeys I've made, the twenty-six and half times up and down Richmond Beach. If you know that hill, its insane. My walk from Shoreline to north Lynnwood and my walk from West Seattle through White Center to downtown at midnight, crazy in itself, that last one was desperation to get home though. These walks form a motivation for a finish rather than the thought of the destination. It also gives me the opportunity to interact with the people around me as opposed to me flying by them at a high rate of speed, waving. It helps me as well knowing and mentally marking the distances I was able to reach and the time it took to reach the destination. Often its much faster than I expect because I walk like most people run.

People often ask to walk with me, but I'm a bit hesitant to agree because I like my pace. It changes, and I like to switch it up carelessly sometimes. I look angry, but I'm not. I'm actually preparing myself mentally to take off. Also I may be in severe pain at the beginning. It all depends on what stage I'm at when you see me. The moment my endorphins are released my pace kicks up, and it'll be hard to stop me. Pain follows post workout, but I prefer pain because of activity as opposed to pain because of sitting or being inactive. My body earned the pain.

The Ultimate Stare

—⁓—

I've found over the years that people have a serious issue with staring at me. I find it quite hilarious at times because their eyes and face are trying to figure out what's wrong with me. It becomes an annoyance, like what are you staring at, take a picture while you're at it, or ask. The staring that you're doing right now is more rude and disrespectful than if you simply just asked. It's like were in third grade all over again and its mostly grown people.

I hear complaints from women getting stared at and I wonder what they would do if they had my body and walked down the street? I can't compare it to my situation because I don't know them and they don't know me. It's funny to see them after I ask them "what's up?" because all of them jump, not physically but you get the idea.

My advice to you if you seriously have questions, just freaking ask. Staring just prolongs your curiosity and increases the likelihood of you falling on your face, walking into a wall, one leg trips over the other sometimes, and sometimes, one leg is turned in kind of like one clubbed foot due to weakness. In other parts of the country, when you stare it often means you want to fight, you have a problem, but often times those questions are asked and it's dealt with. But if you've never been in that situation before, of course you wouldn't know that.

Dreams are Attainable if You Believe

—ɷ—

When I was younger I had simple dreams, not sure if they'd come to fruition due to my life being heavily consumed with doctors' appointments, physical therapists, neurologists, and so on. Making decisions based off of the current situation, no one knew I would completely obliterate the limitations of their knowledge. I didn't even know, but I'll tell you I wasn't a fan of what they had to say. I felt totally controlled, and it was as if I tried to do something outside the recommendation, something seriously catastrophic would happen. Well even though I was smart at a young age, I was stubborn, but that stubbornness was the one of the things that started a mindset to need to prove your findings before I follow what you have to say when it comes to any healing timeline or process.

They often gave me a timeline that they give to everyone. I'm not like everyone else, my body isn't like everyone else's, and chances are I have more metal in my body than most. I do things outside the norm and it has worked to this point, so I must be doing something right. I've been able to reach so many things that others put outside my reach, sometimes because it was outside of theirs. In most cases they were making a decision to the best of their knowledge, which I can respect but at the same time I have my history of overcoming the odds.

The Effects of Disease

—⁓—

From the time I can remember I've seen it. Cancer, Alzheimer's, dementia, I've heard of them but never had to deal with them or battle them, but I did experience the horrendous effects slowly take away people extremely close to me. Some were able to beat it, and some with that same courage and determination were not. This is another reason I'd like to shine a light on these diseases. We are currently on the road to defeating each of these, but for those whom haven't gotten to see the result, it is extremely devastating to all involved. I have been witness to the effects of lung cancer, in which my grandpa suffered, all the way to the Alzheimer's, that took a close friend's parent. It has placed a humbleness and vision to sustain positives for not only those fighting it currently but for the families of those gone to soon.

I had the honor to be in many lives who fought hard and have lost. But I have hope that change is on its way for those currently facing this battle. I hope you feel empowered to continue your fight and remember you're not alone and your battle isn't for nothing. You are creating change in the development of treatments for those who are in the same predicament. You are changing the lives of so many, and I applaud your strength. Watching it firsthand was hard, but I encourage those who are in charge of care to remember this isn't your fault. This isn't in your control, and the fact you're taking the responsibility of care is to be applauded. Stay strong, you are not alone.

David

When I first got really into running in Shoreline, I would be out every day. He would always have a smile on his face and honk his horn in his what I thought very nice BMW or on his bike. He was one of the first people I really got to know because he took the time to talk. He excelled at sports as well. One day he invited me to play basketball. It was a good time, then I'd watch him from the sidelines play football during an annual turkey bowl with some of the coolest peeps whom later I got to know quite well. I was always going running or walking, but he would always wave or take the effort to say what's up. One day I got to stop and talk to him. He was one of the nicest people I've ever met, and it wasn't just me he had a huge impact on. First becoming a life guard, he later progressed and became an AMR. It was a powerful statement and just reflects the dedication to his work and the people surrounding him.

He was one of those people who fits into any setting, and unfortunately he was taken from us way before his time in a motorcycle accident. It was hard to adjust not seeing him every day on his bike or in his car. It seemed so unreal, as the realization came it became harder to come to grips with it. To his friends he was an amazing person to be around, a caring, compassionate person and was always there when you needed a hand or to help. You will be missed David, your spirit and kindness will live in the hearts of everyone you touched and impacted. We lost a kind soul but gained an amazing spirit that I know myself and others will never forget.

The Impossible and Thinking

—ᗰ—

Over many years the word impossible was said to me, but I failed to realize that most of the people saying those things were either trying to protect my hopes and not getting them up, or their style of thinking didn't mesh with mine. Thankfully, I was able to break the barriers that they placed upon me.

No one expected a comeback powerful enough to defy the thinking of someone who has a degree, and I'm not downing the education obtained, but the mindset and critical thinking of the person is key to the ability to potentially overcome the battle or challenge. Sometimes a little motivation and a little thinking outside the box can create an expanded inspiration of thinking and up-lift the mind battling the challenge placed in front of them. If you find yourself feeling a sense of doubt, remember to focus on what you can control and take what you can and challenge yourself to learn a way to adapt. You are worth the effort. Doubt hasn't earned its rightful place, and I encourage you to expand beyond the boundaries so that you no longer see them.

Life and Its Twists and Turns

—⚮—

My life and journey has been one of highlights, and in the eyes of many, near impossible obstacles. Thus far, it's been filled with some life changing events both positive and negative, but the positive has been much more consistent. Through the process of not only writing this but becoming a vision of inspiration to others, many have not made it to this point or been able to see the highlights of their own highlights and accomplishments both in progress and completed.

I strive every day to make the best out of every situation because I know how short life can be. I encourage you to continue your efforts in whatever it is you seek to accomplish. It can sometimes be a mental game where you may be physically ready but mentally you're stuck. Just remember there is always opportunity to try again but your first attempt could be the only one you need to jumpstart your vision. Walking and running has been at the forefront of my journey due to the fact that the ability has been taken from me a little over five times, but the vision itself was safe. I knew I could try again because mentally I was ready. The opportunity is yours, the time in which you have to accomplish it is unknown, but as long as you're doing what you love and reaching towards it, you are well on your way to being a success story.

Seattle Magazine

The following excerpt is from the *Seattle Magazine* article, "How a Boy With a Crippling Injury Became Shoreline's Inspirational 'Running Man'" by Stephen Strom (November, 2018):

It's easy to pick out Lamont Thomas' booming voice in the crowded Café Aroma. His laugh carries through the Shoreline coffee shop, drowning the buzz of people and clinking mugs. Thomas, sporting his favorite Julius "Dr. J" Erving jersey, lets his long legs hang loosely off the stool and grins infectiously.

He wears many hats: mentor, comedian, businessman, writer, runner. But as someone who was once told he'd never walk again, it's the last one that has Thomas beaming with pride.

"I like Richmond Beach," he says of his favorite running spot. "It's like a present afterwards. You go

down to the beach, you look at it for a second, and you're like, 'I made it,' and then you run back."

Perhaps better known in Shoreline as "The Running Man," Thomas, who turns 30 at the end of this month, released his autobiography co-written with Ashley M. Graham this spring. The book begins the day a 2-year-old Thomas was hit by a car, launching him into the air before coming down on the rough pavement. The collision left him with extensive injuries including broken limbs, a shattered skull and severe brain trauma. Thomas would need a miracle to survive.

Fortunately, a nearby doctor performed CPR until paramedics arrived and transported him to Harborview. Still, doctors believed he'd never walk again given the amount of brain trauma he experienced. The road to recovery would be the fight of his life.

After the accident, Thomas was partially paralyzed on his right side and was fit with a plastic vest and halo to prevent further damage to his neck and jaw. He was initially confined to a wheelchair, dealing with scoliosis, but eventually learned to walk using a four-wheeled walker.

Thomas spent his childhood in and out of hospitals, battling self-doubt, bullies and feeling left out. His scoliosis kept him from childhood activities most kids take for granted.

"I basically said look, you want to hurt, I'll give you a reason to. So, I started walking on it. Of course, it was painful," Thomas says, recalling those first steps. "My back was stressed; my scoliosis was stressed. ... I got addicted to pain because I wanted to be outside so bad, that I got used to it."

To this day, Thomas deals with constant pain throughout his body as a result of the accident. But learning to walk again has been worth the pain.

Through extensive therapy and the thrill of proving people wrong, he was able to ditch the walker at age 16. Over time and constantly pushing himself he turned his walk into a run. His body is still more susceptible to injury than most his age, but he now clocks 84 miles a week.

His book, *The Running Miracle*, chronicles his early-life obstacles and others he's face after relearning to walk, like how he's always replacing his shoes because his right leg drags when he walks or runs.

Thomas has been in the spotlight before with an NPR interview, a *Los Angeles Times* profile. He's proud to share his story, acknowledging important people who helped him along the way, including his elementary school gym teacher, Royages Easton, who believed Thomas could do whatever he put his mind to, walker or no. It still motivates Thomas.

For Thomas, his book it's more than sharing his

life moments. "This whole thing in the book is try-
ing to inspire the kids and people that have been told
otherwise," he says. "If my story can inspire a purpose
for you or what I've been through can help you reach
your dream, I'm doing something right."

Thomas' incredible journey is about giving
strength to those that feel they don't have any.

"When I'm walking and running I'm always
in pain. But the fact kids are watching, people are
watching and they're so happy and inspired when
they see me, it makes me happy. That's my endorphin
high. Other than walking, seeing people smile and
giving them hope.

More about Lamont J. Thomas

Lamont J. Thomas would like to connect with his readers through any of the communication channels listed below. Feel free to reach out to him to ask questions or share your thoughts about his story. If your organization would like to invite Mr. Thomas to speak to a group of students or employees, please contact him by phone or email.

Cell Phone:
206-902-8729

Email:
Lamontthomasseattle@gmail.com

Facebook:
/lamont.thomas.5/

Facebook Fan Page:
/lamonttheshorelinerunningmanthomas/

Twitter
@lamonttherunner

For more information about this publication, go to:

www.wardstreetpress.com

colophon

This book is set in JANSON TEXT, an old style font designed by the Hungarian punch cutter Miklós Kis in 1685. The modern day digital version is based on Hermann Zaph's work at Stemple Foundry, where he found the original matrices created by Miklós Kis. *The Walking Miracle* will share this beautiful and enduring typeface.

WARD STREET PRESS
SEATTLE, WASHINGTON

WWW.WARDSTREETPRESS.COM

Made in the USA
Monee, IL
27 August 2020

40106479R00090